Truelife Trivia

Ariana Grande

300 Trivia Questions and Fun Facts

BY BRYSEN HOLTZ

Truelife Trivia Series

Truelife Trivia: Ariana Grande 300 Trivia Questions and Fun Facts. Truelife Trivia Series
Truelife Trivia an imprint of TLM Media LLC

ISBN-13: 979-8-88700-605-5

1. Her rise reflects which quality?

    A. Resilience

    B. Flashiness

    C. Speed only

    D. Comedy

2. What did Ed Sheeran say about Ariana?

    A. Outstanding

    B. Superb

    C. Incredible

    D. Fantastic

3. Her peer reputation is?

    A. Positive

    B. Mixed

    C. Negative

    D. Unknown

4. What is Ariana's most followed social?

    A. Instagram

    B. Twitter

    C. Facebook

    D. Snapchat

5. What did Demi Lovato say about Ariana?

A. Fierce

B. Brilliant

C. Inventive

D. Resourceful

6. What did Halsey say about Ariana?

A. Unbelievable

B. Astounding

C. Incredible

D. Amazing

7. What was Ariana's first Billboard award?

A. Top Female Artist

B. Top New Artist

C. Top Album

D. Top Song

8. What is Ariana's most loved charity?

A. One Love Manchester

B. Grande Relief

C. Ariana Aid

D. Charity Gala

9. What was Ariana's favorite song?

    A. My Heart Will Go On

    B. Imagine

    C. Thriller

    D. Like a Prayer

10. Ariana Grande avoids public feuds?

    A. Yes mostly

    B. No often

    C. Unknown

    D. Rarely

11. Fans learn about her youth through?

    A. Talk shows

    B. Reality TV

    C. Leaks

    D. Music videos

12. What was Ariana's first sold-out tour?

    A. Honeymoon

    B. My Everything

    C. Dangerous Woman

    D. Sweetener

13. What is Ariana's favorite holiday?

    A. Christmas
    B. Easter
    C. New Year
    D. Thanksgiving

14. Ariana Grande avoided what during her rise?

    A. Controversy
    B. Training
    C. Opportunities
    D. Publicity

15. What did Selena Gomez say about Ariana?

    A. Wonderful
    B. Marvelous
    C. Outstanding
    D. Splendid

16. What was Ariana's first music video?

    A. The Way
    B. Problem
    C. Break Free
    D. Bang Bang

17. When did Ariana's first album release?

    A. 2013

    B. 2014

    C. 2015

    D. 2016

18. Who is Ariana's husband?

    A. Dalton

    B. David

    C. Tom

    D. Mark

19. What was Ariana's favorite movie?

    A. Titanic

    B. Avatar

    C. Inception

    D. The Notebook

20. What is Ariana's favorite candy?

    A. Chocolate

    B. Gummy Bears

    C. Jelly Beans

    D. Lollipop

21. Fans say she earned success by?

A. Hard work

B. Trends

C. Scandals

D. Sponsors

22. What did Billie Eilish say about Ariana?

A. Inspirational

B. Visionary

C. Creative

D. Artistic

23. What is Ariana's favorite book?

A. Harry Potter

B. 1984

C. LOTR

D. Hobbit

24. What is Ariana's favorite sport?

A. Basketball

B. Football

C. Swimming

D. Tennis

25. Who is Ariana's favorite athlete?

A. Serena

B. LeBron

C. Usain

D. Michael

26. She describes her upbringing as?

A. Creative

B. Strict

C. Chaotic

D. Isolated

27. What did John Legend say about Ariana?

A. Terrific

B. Wonderful

C. Marvelous

D. Splendid

28. Ariana Grande is admired for what skill?

A. Vocal range

B. Dancing

C. Directing

D. Comedy

29. When did Ariana host SNL?

    A. 2014

    B. 2015

    C. 2016

    D. 2017

30. What is Ariana's favorite TV show?

    A. Friends

    B. GOT

    C. Stranger Things

    D. Glee

31. Ariana Grande is known for being?

    A. Soft spoken

    B. Flashy

    C. Extravagant

    D. Showy

32. What did Mariah Carey say about Ariana?

    A. Amazing

    B. Good

    C. Bad

    D. Average

33. Fun interviews show Ariana Grande is?

    A. Quick witted
    B. Serious only
    C. Detached
    D. Awkward

34. What was Ariana's first magazine cover?

    A. Vogue
    B. Elle
    C. Cosmo
    D. Seventeen

35. Media portrayal of Ariana Grande is?

    A. Balanced
    B. Sensational
    C. Negative
    D. Biased

36. Ariana Grande foes are usually?

    A. Media narratives
    B. Personal rivals
    C. Legal enemies
    D. Public figures

37. Who is Ariana's childhood friend?

    A. Courtney
    B. Alexa
    C. Liz
    D. Gillian

38. Her upbringing helped her stay?

    A. Disciplined
    B. Flashy
    C. Detached
    D. Competitive

39. What is Ariana's favorite movie?

    A. Titanic
    B. Avatar
    C. Inception
    D. The Notebook

40. Her milestones show Ariana Grande as?

    A. Evolving
    B. Stagnant
    C. Unfocused
    D. Overexposed

41. Birthplace pride connects Ariana Grande to?

    A. Her roots
    B. Studios only
    C. Awards shows
    D. Labels

42. What was Ariana's first No.1 hit?

    A. The Way
    B. Problem
    C. Break Free
    D. Thank U Next

43. What is Ariana's birth season?

    A. Winter
    B. Spring
    C. Summer
    D. Fall

44. Fans enjoy her humor because it is?

    A. Playful
    B. Loud
    C. Chaotic
    D. Slapstick

45. Fun facts trend about her on?

   A. Fan pages

   B. Finance feeds

   C. Weather sites

   D. Alerts

46. What did Taylor Swift say about Ariana?

   A. Sweet

   B. Brave

   C. Awesome

   D. Creative

47. What is Ariana's favorite song?

   A. Imagine

   B. My Heart Will Go On

   C. Thriller

   D. Like a Prayer

48. Who is Ariana's pet dog?

   A. Toulouse

   B. Max

   C. Charlie

   D. Buddy

49. What did Madonna say about Ariana?

    A. Gifted
    B. Determined
    C. Passionate
    D. Innovative

50. What was Ariana's favorite toy?

    A. Doll
    B. Teddy Bear
    C. Car
    D. Blocks

51. What is Ariana's birth weight?

    A. 5 lbs
    B. 6 lbs
    C. 7 lbs
    D. 8 lbs

52. What is Ariana's birth animal?

    A. Rabbit
    B. Tiger
    C. Dragon
    D. Snake

53. What city was Ariana born in?

A. Miami

B. Boca Raton

C. Orlando

D. Tampa

54. Who is Ariana's favorite chef?

A. Gordon

B. Rachel

C. Bobby

D. Jamie

55. What is Ariana's favorite director?

A. Steven

B. Quentin

C. James

D. Christopher

56. Who is Ariana's favorite singer?

A. Mariah

B. Whitney

C. Celine

D. Madonna

57. Her fun moments appear during?

A. Behind scenes

B. Talk shows

C. Sports events

D. Ads

58. What is Ariana's birth star sign?

A. Pisces

B. Aries

C. Leo

D. Virgo

59. Ariana Grande handles rumors with?

A. Silence

B. Anger

C. Sarcasm

D. Statements

60. Fans describe her journey as?

A. Authentic

B. Calculated

C. Chaotic

D. Accidental

61. What is Ariana's nationality?

    A. Canadian

    B. British

    C. American

    D. Australian

62. What is Ariana's most successful movie?

    A. The Lorax

    B. Swindle

    C. Zoolander 2

    D. Scream Queens

63. Global fans view her as?

    A. Authentic

    B. Manufactured

    C. Trend based

    D. Ephemeral

64. What was Ariana's favorite sport?

    A. Soccer

    B. Basketball

    C. Swimming

    D. Running

65. What was Ariana's breakout hit?

    A. The Way
    B. Problem
    C. Break Free
    D. Bang Bang

66. What was Ariana's first album?

    A. Yours Truly
    B. My Everything
    C. Dangerous Woman
    D. Sweetener

67. What is Ariana's favorite food?

    A. Pizza
    B. Pasta
    C. Burger
    D. Sushi

68. What was Ariana's first TV appearance?

    A. Victorious
    B. Sam & Cat
    C. The Voice
    D. The Ellen Show

69. Critics note her milestone choices are?

A. Intentional

B. Random

C. Commercial

D. Forced

70. Ariana Grande recent milestones include?

A. New albums

B. Film awards

C. Brand exits

D. Politics

71. When did Ariana win her first Grammy?

A. 2019

B. 2020

C. 2021

D. 2022

72. What is Ariana's most viewed video?

A. The Way

B. Problem

C. Break Free

D. Bang Bang

73. Ariana Grande rise is described as?

    A. Transformative
    B. Accidental
    C. Manufactured
    D. Sudden

74. What is Ariana's favorite drink?

    A. Water
    B. Coffee
    C. Tea
    D. Juice

75. Birth trivia of Ariana Grande resurfaces when?

    A. New releases
    B. Elections
    C. Sports finals
    D. Tech launches

76. What was Ariana's favorite drink?

    A. Water
    B. Coffee
    C. Tea
    D. Juice

77. What was Ariana's first charity concert?

    A. One Love Manchester

    B. Ariana Aid

    C. Grande Relief

    D. Charity Gala

78. What is Ariana's favorite movie?

    A. Titanic

    B. Avatar

    C. Inception

    D. The Notebook

79. Who is Ariana's brother?

    A. Frankie

    B. Michael

    C. John

    D. David

80. What is Ariana's most popular song?

    A. Thank U Next

    B. Problem

    C. Break Free

    D. Bang Bang

81. What is Ariana's most popular perfume?

   A. Ari

   B. Cloud

   C. Thank U Next

   D. Sweet Like Candy

82. Ariana Grande values what in partners?

   A. Respect

   B. Fame

   C. Control

   D. Publicity

83. Fans discuss Ariana Grande birthplace on?

   A. Fan pages

   B. Legal sites

   C. Music charts

   D. Tech blogs

84. Co stars praise Ariana Grande for?

   A. Professionalism

   B. Ego

   C. Silence

   D. Competition

85. Who is Ariana's best friend?

   A. Courtney

   B. Alexa

   C. Liz

   D. Gillian

86. What was Ariana's first book?

   A. Moonlight

   B. Autobiography

   C. My Story

   D. Diary

87. What was Ariana's first movie?

   A. The Lorax

   B. Swindle

   C. Scream Queens

   D. Zoolander 2

88. What was Ariana's favorite food?

   A. Pizza

   B. Pasta

   C. Burger

   D. Sushi

89. When did Ariana's first tour start?

    A. 2015

    B. 2016

    C. 2017

    D. 2018

90. Who is Ariana's husband?

    A. Dalton

    B. David

    C. Tom

    D. Mark

91. Who is Ariana's favorite writer?

    A. JK Rowling

    B. Stephen King

    C. George RR Martin

    D. Agatha Christie

92. What was Ariana's first TV show?

    A. Victorious

    B. Sam & Cat

    C. The Voice

    D. The Ellen Show

93. What is Ariana's favorite candy?

    A. Chocolate

    B. Gummy Bears

    C. Jelly Beans

    D. Lollipop

94. Who is Ariana's best girl friend?

    A. Victoria

    B. Courtney

    C. Liz

    D. Alexa

95. Who is Ariana's favorite photographer?

    A. Mario

    B. Annie

    C. David

    D. Peter

96. What did Beyonce say about Ariana?

    A. Powerful

    B. Elegant

    C. Graceful

    D. Charming

97. What is Ariana's favorite TV show?

A. Friends

B. GOT

C. Stranger Things

D. Glee

98. Fans celebrate Ariana Grande birth facts with?

A. Online posts

B. Brand sales

C. Stock trades

D. Game events

99. Ariana Grande nationality discussed in?

A. Recent interviews

B. Ads

C. Music lyrics

D. Podcasts ads

100. What is Ariana's favorite ice cream?

A. Vanilla

B. Chocolate

C. Strawberry

D. Mint

101. What did The Weeknd say about Ariana?

A. Spectacular

B. Sensational

C. Remarkable

D. Fantastic

102. Who is Ariana's celebrity crush?

A. Leonardo

B. Brad

C. Johnny

D. Tom

103. Who is Ariana's favorite sibling?

A. Frankie

B. Michael

C. John

D. David

104. What is Ariana's birth lunar phase?

A. Full

B. New

C. Waning

D. Waxing

105. Fans revisit birth info due to?

    A. Curiosity

    B. Scandals

    C. Legal cases

    D. Marketing

106. What is Ariana's favorite actor?

    A. Leonardo

    B. Brad

    C. Johnny

    D. Tom

107. Ariana Grande current image is?

    A. Private

    B. Reclusive

    C. Scandal driven

    D. Unfocused

108. Ariana Grande recalls school years as?

    A. Formative

    B. Dull

    C. Negative

    D. Irrelevant

109. What is Ariana's favorite book?

A. Harry Potter
B. 1984
C. LOTR
D. Hobbit

110. Her continued rise depends on?

A. Creative control
B. Marketing stunts
C. Trends only
D. Virality

111. What is Ariana's birth tarot card?

A. The Fool
B. The Magician
C. The Star
D. The Moon

112. What was Ariana's first award?

A. Grammy
B. Billboard
C. MTV
D. Teen Choice

113. Fans highlight which milestone most?

  A. Artistic evolution

  B. Debut only

  C. Retirement

  D. Scandals

114. Audiences describe Ariana Grande as?

  A. Authentic

  B. Artificial

  C. Detached

  D. Overacted

115. World perception of Ariana Grande is?

  A. Stable

  B. Evolving

  C. Chaotic

  D. Polarizing

116. Ariana Grande is often described as?

  A. Dedicated

  B. Reckless

  C. Detached

  D. Unpredictable

117. What did Justin Bieber say about Ariana?

    A. Talented

    B. Beautiful

    C. Smart

    D. Funny

118. What is Ariana's birthstone?

    A. Ruby

    B. Amethyst

    C. Sapphire

    D. Diamond

119. When did Ariana's first book release?

    A. 2013

    B. 2014

    C. 2015

    D. 2016

120. Recent chats show Ariana Grande was?

    A. Driven

    B. Rebellious

    C. Aggressive

    D. Withdrawn

121. Ariana Grande avoids sharing?

   A. Private moments

   B. Performances

   C. Awards

   D. Releases

122. Her milestones confirm longevity?

   A. Yes clearly

   B. No doubtful

   C. Unknown

   D. Never

123. What hospital was Ariana born in?

   A. North Shore

   B. Memorial West

   C. Baptist

   D. St. Mary's

124. When did Ariana start her career?

   A. 2008

   B. 2009

   C. 2010

   D. 2011

125. What is Ariana's most liked photo?

    A. Selfie
    B. Concert
    C. Dog
    D. Vacation

126. What was Ariana's first tour?

    A. Honeymoon
    B. My Everything
    C. Dangerous Woman
    D. Sweetener

127. Industry views her rise as?

    A. Deserved
    B. Forced
    C. Temporary
    D. Overhyped

128. What was Ariana's favorite singer?

    A. Mariah Carey
    B. Whitney Houston
    C. Celine Dion
    D. Madonna

129. Fans admire her honesty about?

   A. Personal growth

   B. Drama

   C. Conflict

   D. Public feuds

130. Ariana Grande enjoys what off stage?

   A. Quiet time

   B. Extreme sports

   C. Gaming

   D. Cooking shows

131. What is Ariana's middle name?

   A. Joan

   B. Marie

   C. Lyn

   D. Ann

132. What is Ariana's most streamed song?

   A. Thank U Next

   B. Problem

   C. Break Free

   D. Bang Bang

133. Ariana Grande gained renewed attention through?

    A. New music
    B. Reality shows
    C. Ads
    D. Tours only

134. Ariana Grande is described as what artist?

    A. Pop vocalist
    B. Rapper
    C. DJ
    D. Producer only

135. What did Shawn Mendes say about Ariana?

    A. Magnificent
    B. Remarkable
    C. Extraordinary
    D. Spectacular

136. What is Ariana's favorite holiday?

    A. Christmas
    B. Easter
    C. New Year
    D. Thanksgiving

137. Who is Ariana's favorite niece?

    A. Lani
    B. Nicole
    C. Sarah
    D. Jamie

138. Who is Ariana's father?

    A. Edward
    B. David
    C. John
    D. Robert

139. Fans relate to her growth because?

    A. Honest
    B. Elite
    C. Mysterious
    D. Unusual

140. Ariana Grande birthday trends on?

    A. Social media
    B. Finance news
    C. Weather apps
    D. Stock reports

141. Her global appeal comes from?

   A. Emotional connection
   B. Marketing
   C. Scandals
   D. Virality

142. Ariana Grande is respected for?

   A. Artistry
   B. Virality
   C. Brand deals
   D. Trends

143. What is Ariana's favorite ice cream?

   A. Vanilla
   B. Chocolate
   C. Strawberry
   D. Mint

144. Who is Ariana's favorite dancer?

   A. Michael
   B. Janet
   C. Chris
   D. Usher

145. What time was Ariana born?

    A. 8:45 AM
    B. 9:30 PM
    C. 7:00 AM
    D. 10:00 PM

146. What is Ariana's birthdate?

    A. June 26 1993
    B. March 25 1994
    C. April 10 1993
    D. March 25 1993

147. Ariana Grande birth stories appear in?

    A. Fan discussions
    B. Weather news
    C. Finance feeds
    D. Ads

148. Who is Ariana's favorite aunt?

    A. Lani
    B. Nicole
    C. Sarah
    D. Jamie

149. Who is Ariana's first kiss?

A. Graham

B. David

C. John

D. Peter

150. What was Ariana's first song release?

A. The Way

B. Problem

C. Break Free

D. Bang Bang

151. What was Ariana's first perfume?

A. Ari

B. Cloud

C. Thank U Next

D. Sweet Like Candy

152. Ariana Grande early interests included?

A. Performing arts

B. Finance

C. Politics

D. Sports only

153. Who is Ariana's manager?

    A. Scooter
    B. David
    C. John
    D. Mark

154. What was Ariana's first acting award?

    A. Best Actress
    B. Best Supporting
    C. Best Newcomer
    D. Best Young Actress

155. Ariana Grande chooses projects that are?

    A. Personal
    B. Random
    C. Commercial only
    D. Accidental

156. Media calls Ariana Grande?

    A. Influential
    B. Unreliable
    C. Overexposed
    D. Chaotic

157. What is Ariana's most retweeted tweet?

A. Song

B. Quote

C. Selfie

D. Video

158. Who is Ariana's favorite actor?

A. Leonardo

B. Brad

C. Johnny

D. Tom

159. Recent media credits her rise to?

A. Talent

B. Luck alone

C. Virality

D. Nepotism

160. Critics note Ariana Grande growth as?

A. Mature

B. Stagnant

C. Declining

D. Unclear

161. Ariana Grande defines love with?

A. Care

B. Control

C. Power

D. Attention

162. Friends call Ariana Grande a?

A. Loyal ally

B. Lone wolf

C. Disruptor

D. Scene stealer

163. What did Bruno Mars say about Ariana?

A. Awesome

B. Phenomenal

C. Fantastic

D. Superb

164. What did Camila Cabello say about Ariana?

A. Admirable

B. Impressive

C. Remarkable

D. Extraordinary

165. What is Ariana's favorite dessert?

    A. Ice Cream
    B. Pie
    C. Cake
    D. Brownie

166. What is Ariana's birth Chinese element?

    A. Fire
    B. Earth
    C. Water
    D. Wood

167. What is Ariana's most famous hairstyle?

    A. Ponytail
    B. Bob
    C. Braids
    D. Curls

168. Who is Ariana's favorite painter?

    A. Van Gogh
    B. Picasso
    C. Da Vinci
    D. Monet

169. Fans say Ariana Grande laughs easily?

    A. Yes often
    B. Rarely
    C. Never
    D. Unknown

170. What was Ariana's first endorsement?

    A. Reebok
    B. Nike
    C. Puma
    D. Adidas

171. What is Ariana's birth lucky number?

    A. 3
    B. 7
    C. 9
    D. 11

172. Who is Ariana's favorite historian?

    A. Herodotus
    B. Thucydides
    C. Plutarch
    D. Polybius

173. Who are Ariana's parents?

A. Joan & Edward

B. Marie & David

C. Ann & John

D. Lisa & Robert

174. What was Ariana's first platinum album?

A. Yours Truly

B. My Everything

C. Dangerous Woman

D. Sweetener

175. Who is Ariana's favorite cousin?

A. Lani

B. Nicole

C. Sarah

D. Jamie

176. What is Ariana's most famous collaboration?

A. The Weeknd

B. Nicki Minaj

C. Drake

D. Justin Bieber

177. Recent milestones brought Ariana Grande?

A. New listeners

B. Backlash

C. Legal issues

D. Retirement talk

178. Ariana Grande handles criticism with?

A. Reflection

B. Anger

C. Mockery

D. Defensiveness

179. What is Ariana's birth planet?

A. Mars

B. Venus

C. Saturn

D. Jupiter

180. Milestones are discussed at?

A. Fan events

B. Stock meetings

C. Weather briefings

D. Ads

181. Who is Ariana's ex-fiance?

A. Pete

B. Justin

C. Shawn

D. Nathan

182. Ariana Grande keeps personal life?

A. Selective

B. Public

C. Secretive

D. Documented

183. What is Ariana's most iconic music video?

A. The Way

B. Problem

C. Break Free

D. Bang Bang

184. What did Drake say about Ariana?

A. Genius

B. Innovative

C. Groundbreaking

D. Exceptional

185. What is Ariana's most famous tour?

    A. Honeymoon
    B. Sweetener
    C. Dangerous Woman
    D. My Everything

186. What is Ariana's favorite animal?

    A. Dog
    B. Cat
    C. Bird
    D. Fish

187. What is Ariana's most sold album?

    A. Sweetener
    B. My Everything
    C. Dangerous Woman
    D. Yours Truly

188. Audiences trust her creative choices?

    A. Yes strongly
    B. No rarely
    C. Unknown
    D. Sometimes

189. What was Ariana's first MTV award?

  A. Best New Artist

  B. Best Pop Video

  C. Best Collaboration

  D. Best Female Artist

190. What is Ariana's favorite animal?

  A. Cat

  B. Dog

  C. Rabbit

  D. Horse

191. Ariana Grande is active mainly in?

  A. Music

  B. Politics

  C. Modeling

  D. Journalism

192. What did Nicki Minaj say about Ariana?

  A. Phenomenal

  B. Amazing

  C. Unstoppable

  D. Fantastic

193. Ariana Grande birth facts remain?

A. Relevant

B. Forgotten

C. Hidden

D. Disputed

194. Who is Ariana's favorite scientist?

A. Einstein

B. Newton

C. Hawking

D. Curie

195. Ariana Grande influence is strongest in?

A. Pop music

B. Film awards

C. Sports media

D. Fashion weeks

196. What was Ariana's first charity event?

A. One Love Manchester

B. Ariana Aid

C. Grande Relief

D. Charity Gala

197. What is Ariana's most awarded album?

A. Sweetener

B. My Everything

C. Dangerous Woman

D. Yours Truly

198. What was Ariana's first hobby?

A. Singing

B. Dancing

C. Painting

D. Reading

199. What is Ariana's birth year sign?

A. Horse

B. Goat

C. Monkey

D. Rat

200. Who is Ariana's rival?

A. Selena

B. Taylor

C. Miley

D. Katy

201. What was Ariana's first performance?

A. School Play

B. Talent Show

C. Concert

D. TV Show

202. What was Ariana's first fashion award?

A. Vogue

B. Fashion Icon

C. Best Dressed

D. Style Star

203. The world sees Ariana Grande as?

A. Influential

B. Overrated

C. Irrelevant

D. Controversial

204. What did Katy Perry say about Ariana?

A. Strong

B. Unique

C. Kind

D. Caring

205. What is Ariana's favorite flower?

A. Rose

B. Lily

C. Daisy

D. Tulip

206. Who is Ariana's favorite uncle?

A. Frank

B. James

C. Robert

D. William

207. What was Ariana's first pet?

A. Dog

B. Cat

C. Bird

D. Fish

208. What is Ariana's favorite sport?

A. Swimming

B. Running

C. Soccer

D. Basketball

209. Ariana Grande recent work focuses on?

    A. Music projects
    B. Talk shows
    C. Sports events
    D. Game streams

210. What is Ariana's birth flower?

    A. Rose
    B. Lily
    C. Daisy
    D. Sunflower

211. Public sees her relationships as?

    A. Evolving
    B. Chaotic
    C. Scandalous
    D. Unclear

212. What is Ariana's favorite color?

    A. Red
    B. Blue
    C. Pink
    D. Purple

213. What is Ariana's zodiac sign?

    A. Libra

    B. Scorpio

    C. Virgo

    D. Cancer

214. What is Ariana's favorite designer?

    A. Chanel

    B. Dior

    C. Gucci

    D. Versace

215. Ariana Grande is best known as?

    A. Songwriter

    B. TV host

    C. Director only

    D. Producer only

216. What was Ariana's first fan club?

    A. Arianators

    B. Grande Fans

    C. AG Club

    D. Ariana Nation

217. What was Ariana's favorite activity?

A. Drawing

B. Dancing

C. Singing

D. Playing

218. What was Ariana's first social media post?

A. Selfie

B. Song

C. Video

D. Quote

219. What is Ariana's most famous quote?

A. Be Yourself

B. Stay Strong

C. Love Yourself

D. Keep Going

220. What is Ariana's favorite singer?

A. Whitney

B. Michael

C. Madonna

D. Janet

221. What is Ariana's most watched interview?

A. Ellen

B. Jimmy Fallon

C. Oprah

D. James Corden

222. What did Rihanna say about Ariana?

A. Inspiring

B. Powerful

C. Charismatic

D. Dynamic

223. Who is Ariana's first boyfriend?

A. Graham

B. David

C. John

D. Peter

224. What is Ariana Grande known for today?

A. Acting only

B. Singing career

C. Reality TV

D. Fashion design

225. Peers describe Ariana Grande as?

   A. Professional

   B. Unpredictable

   C. Harsh

   D. Detached

226. Who is Ariana's favorite sculptor?

   A. Michelangelo

   B. Donatello

   C. Leonardo

   D. Raphael

227. Fans respect Ariana Grande for?

   A. Boundaries

   B. Oversharing

   C. Drama posts

   D. Feuds

228. What was Ariana's favorite book?

   A. Harry Potter

   B. 1984

   C. LOTR

   D. Hobbit

229. What is Ariana's favorite hobby?

A. Singing

B. Dancing

C. Drawing

D. Reading

230. What is Ariana's favorite flower?

A. Rose

B. Lily

C. Daisy

D. Tulip

231. Who is Ariana's favorite nephew?

A. Max

B. Charlie

C. David

D. John

232. What is Ariana's favorite color?

A. Pink

B. Blue

C. Red

D. Green

233. What is Ariana's birth year?

    A. 1991

    B. 1992

    C. 1993

    D. 1994

234. What was Ariana's first live performance?

    A. MTV Awards

    B. Billboard Awards

    C. Grammy Awards

    D. Teen Choice Awards

235. When did Ariana's first movie premiere?

    A. 2012

    B. 2013

    C. 2014

    D. 2015

236. What is Ariana's favorite drink?

    A. Water

    B. Coffee

    C. Tea

    D. Juice

237. Who is Ariana's favorite designer?

    A. Chanel
    B. Dior
    C. Gucci
    D. Versace

238. Who is Ariana's ex-fiance?

    A. Pete
    B. Justin
    C. Shawn
    D. Nathan

239. What was Ariana's favorite subject?

    A. Math
    B. Science
    C. History
    D. Art

240. Ariana Grande surprises fans by?

    A. Being candid
    B. Being loud
    C. Being flashy
    D. Being controversial

241. Ariana Grande symbolizes what?

A. Modern pop artistry

B. Internet fame

C. Fashion trends

D. Virality

242. What is Ariana's favorite actress?

A. Jennifer

B. Emma

C. Scarlett

D. Angelina

243. What is Ariana's birth gemstone?

A. Emerald

B. Opal

C. Topaz

D. Peridot

244. Ariana Grande values collaboration over?

A. Ego

B. Control

C. Speed

D. Attention

245. What was Ariana's first song?

    A. The Way

    B. Problem

    C. Break Free

    D. Bang Bang

246. Who is Ariana's godmother?

    A. Gloria

    B. Betty

    C. Denise

    D. Lynn

247. What was Ariana's first role?

    A. Charlotte

    B. Kat

    C. Sam

    D. Emily

248. What is Ariana's natural hair color?

    A. Black

    B. Brown

    C. Blonde

    D. Red

249. What is Ariana Grande's last name?

    A. Voight

    B. Williams

    C. David

    D. Smith

250. What is Ariana's favorite food?

    A. Pasta

    B. Pizza

    C. Burger

    D. Sushi

251. Critics call Ariana Grande performances?

    A. Polished

    B. Messy

    C. Forgettable

    D. Rushed

252. Ariana Grande birth details feel?

    A. Well known

    B. Secretive

    C. Unknown

    D. Manufactured

253. Ariana Grande prefers calm hobbies?

A. Yes
B. No
C. Unknown
D. Never mentioned

254. Ariana Grande milestones shape her?

A. Legacy
B. Finances only
C. Public image only
D. Brand deals

255. What was Ariana's favorite flower?

A. Rose
B. Lily
C. Daisy
D. Tulip

256. What is Ariana's most praised performance?

A. Grammy
B. Billboard
C. MTV
D. Teen Choice

257. Who is Ariana's favorite director?

A. Steven

B. Quentin

C. James

D. Christopher

258. What is Ariana's birth month?

A. March

B. April

C. June

D. August

259. Ariana Grande is known for being?

A. Supportive

B. Confrontational

C. Isolated

D. Competitive

260. Ariana Grande rise inspires?

A. Artists

B. Politicians

C. Athletes

D. Executives

261. Growing up shaped Ariana Grande focus on?

A. Music
B. Fame
C. Sports
D. Politics

262. Industry friendships are mostly?

A. Long term
B. Short lived
C. Transactional
D. Public only

263. Fans admire Ariana Grande for?

A. Consistency
B. Drama
C. Controversy
D. Trends

264. What is Ariana's most viewed concert?

A. Honeymoon
B. Sweetener
C. Dangerous Woman
D. My Everything

265. What is Ariana's most iconic outfit?

A. Red Dress

B. White Gown

C. Black Suit

D. Blue Jeans

266. What was Ariana's favorite game?

A. Hide and Seek

B. Tag

C. Hopscotch

D. Jump Rope

267. Ariana Grande youth influenced her?

A. Vocal style

B. Dancing

C. Directing

D. Writing novels

268. What did Lady Gaga say about Ariana?

A. Exceptional

B. Fantastic

C. Wonderful

D. Remarkable

269. What was Ariana's first instrument?

A. Piano

B. Guitar

C. Violin

D. Drums

270. Where was Ariana Grande born?

A. Florida

B. California

C. Texas

D. New York

271. Ariana Grande legacy is viewed as?

A. Enduring

B. Temporary

C. Unclear

D. Overstated

272. Public says Ariana Grande is?

A. Focused

B. Scattered

C. Unprepared

D. Uncertain

273. Who is Ariana's mother?

A. Joan

B. Marie

C. Ann

D. Lisa

274. Fans note she supports?

A. Fellow artists

B. Rivals

C. Brands

D. Politicians

275. Fans say Ariana Grande vocals are?

A. Powerful

B. Average

C. Flat

D. Untrained

276. Ariana Grande childhood stories appear in?

A. Recent interviews

B. Cartoons

C. Games

D. Ads

277. Who is Ariana's favorite philosopher?

    A. Socrates
    B. Plato
    C. Aristotle
    D. Kant

278. Fans say her fun side feels?

    A. Natural
    B. Forced
    C. Awkward
    D. Scripted

279. What is Ariana's birth lucky color?

    A. Red
    B. Blue
    C. Green
    D. Yellow

280. Who is Ariana's best friend?

    A. Courtney
    B. Alexa
    C. Victoria
    D. Liz

281. What was Ariana's first big break?

    A. Victorious
    B. Sam & Cat
    C. The Voice
    D. The Ellen Show

282. What was Ariana's first school?

    A. Pine Crest
    B. North Broward
    C. American Heritage
    D. University School

283. What is Ariana's favorite dessert?

    A. Cake
    B. Pie
    C. Brownie
    D. Ice Cream

284. Recent articles say she prioritizes?

    A. Emotional health
    B. Career only
    C. Fame growth
    D. Exposure

285. Fans call Ariana Grande a?

A. Pop icon
B. Fashion editor
C. Film critic
D. Reality star

286. Career milestones reflect her?

A. Growth
B. Decline
C. Confusion
D. Repetition

287. What was Ariana's first No.1 album?

A. Yours Truly
B. My Everything
C. Dangerous Woman
D. Sweetener

288. Fans admire Ariana Grande for?

A. Consistency
B. Flashiness
C. Drama
D. Trends

289. What was Ariana's favorite vacation?

    A. Disney World
    B. Beach
    C. Mountains
    D. City

290. Reviewers say Ariana Grande music feels?

    A. Emotional
    B. Empty
    C. Repetitive
    D. Forced

291. What was Ariana's first live TV performance?

    A. MTV Awards
    B. Billboard Awards
    C. Grammy Awards
    D. Teen Choice Awards

292. Where did Ariana grow up?

    A. Florida
    B. California
    C. Texas
    D. New York

293. Who is Ariana's idol?

A. Mariah

B. Whitney

C. Celine

D. Madonna

294. Industry views her milestones as?

A. Well timed

B. Late

C. Rushed

D. Forced

295. Ariana Grande discusses relationships in?

A. Careful interviews

B. Daily vlogs

C. Reality shows

D. Ads

296. What was Ariana's favorite candy?

A. Chocolate

B. Gummy Bears

C. Jelly Beans

D. Lollipop

297. What was Ariana's first fashion line?

    A. AG
    B. Grande Style
    C. Ariana Chic
    D. My Way

298. What was Ariana's first fragrance?

    A. Ari
    B. Cloud
    C. Thank U Next
    D. Sweet Like Candy

299. What was Ariana's first major collaboration?

    A. The Weeknd
    B. Nicki Minaj
    C. Drake
    D. Justin Bieber

300. Who is Ariana's favorite actress?

    A. Jennifer
    B. Emma
    C. Scarlett
    D. Angelina

1. Her rise reflects which quality?

Resilience

2. What did Ed Sheeran say about Ariana?

Outstanding

3. Her peer reputation is?

Positive

4. What is Ariana's most followed social?

Instagram

5. What did Demi Lovato say about Ariana?

Fierce

6. What did Halsey say about Ariana?

Unbelievable

7. What was Ariana's first Billboard award?

Top New Artist

8. What is Ariana's most loved charity?

One Love Manchester

9. What was Ariana's favorite song?

My Heart Will Go On

10. Ariana Grande avoids public feuds?

Yes mostly

11. Fans learn about her youth through?

Talk shows

12. What was Ariana's first sold-out tour?

Honeymoon

13. What is Ariana's favorite holiday?

Christmas

14. Ariana Grande avoided what during her rise?

Controversy

15. What did Selena Gomez say about Ariana?

Wonderful

16. What was Ariana's first music video?

The Way

17. When did Ariana's first album release?

2013

18. Who is Ariana's husband?

Dalton

19. What was Ariana's favorite movie?

Titanic

20. What is Ariana's favorite candy?

Chocolate

21. Fans say she earned success by?

Hard work

22. What did Billie Eilish say about Ariana?

Inspirational

23. What is Ariana's favorite book?

Harry Potter

24. What is Ariana's favorite sport?

Swimming

25. Who is Ariana's favorite athlete?

Serena

26. She describes her upbringing as?

Creative

27. What did John Legend say about Ariana?

Terrific

28. Ariana Grande is admired for what skill?

Vocal range

29. When did Ariana host SNL?

2016

30. What is Ariana's favorite TV show?

Friends

31. Ariana Grande is known for being?

Soft spoken

32. What did Mariah Carey say about Ariana?

Amazing

33. Fun interviews show Ariana Grande is?

Quick witted

34. What was Ariana's first magazine cover?

Seventeen

35. Media portrayal of Ariana Grande is?

Balanced

36. Ariana Grande foes are usually?

Media narratives

37. Who is Ariana's childhood friend?

Alexa

38. Her upbringing helped her stay?

Disciplined

39. What is Ariana's favorite movie?

Titanic

40. Her milestones show Ariana Grande as?

Evolving

41. Birthplace pride connects Ariana Grande to?

Her roots

42. What was Ariana's first No.1 hit?

Thank U Next

43. What is Ariana's birth season?

Spring

44. Fans enjoy her humor because it is?

Playful

45. Fun facts trend about her on?

Fan pages

46. What did Taylor Swift say about Ariana?

Sweet

47. What is Ariana's favorite song?

Imagine

48. Who is Ariana's pet dog?

Toulouse

49. What did Madonna say about Ariana?

Gifted

50. What was Ariana's favorite toy?

Doll

51. What is Ariana's birth weight?

6 lbs

52. What is Ariana's birth animal?

Rabbit

53. What city was Ariana born in?

Boca Raton

54. Who is Ariana's favorite chef?

Gordon

55. What is Ariana's favorite director?

Steven

56. Who is Ariana's favorite singer?

Whitney

57. Her fun moments appear during?

Behind scenes

58. What is Ariana's birth star sign?

Aries

59. Ariana Grande handles rumors with?

Silence

60. Fans describe her journey as?

Authentic

61. What is Ariana's nationality?

American

62. What is Ariana's most successful movie?

The Lorax

63. Global fans view her as?

Authentic

64. What was Ariana's favorite sport?

Swimming

65. What was Ariana's breakout hit?

The Way

66. What was Ariana's first album?

Yours Truly

67. What is Ariana's favorite food?

Pasta

68. What was Ariana's first TV appearance?

Victorious

69. Critics note her milestone choices are?

Intentional

70. Ariana Grande recent milestones include?

New albums

71. When did Ariana win her first Grammy?

2019

72. What is Ariana's most viewed video?

Problem

73. Ariana Grande rise is described as?

Transformative

74. What is Ariana's favorite drink?

Water

75. Birth trivia of Ariana Grande resurfaces when?

New releases

76. What was Ariana's favorite drink?

Water

77. What was Ariana's first charity concert?

One Love Manchester

78. What is Ariana's favorite movie?

Titanic

79. Who is Ariana's brother?

Frankie

80. What is Ariana's most popular song?

Thank U Next

81. What is Ariana's most popular perfume?

Cloud

82. Ariana Grande values what in partners?

Respect

83. Fans discuss Ariana Grande birthplace on?

Fan pages

84. Co stars praise Ariana Grande for?

Professionalism

85. Who is Ariana's best friend?

Alexa

86. What was Ariana's first book?

Moonlight

87. What was Ariana's first movie?

The Lorax

88. What was Ariana's favorite food?

Pasta

89. When did Ariana's first tour start?

2015

90. Who is Ariana's husband?

Dalton

91. Who is Ariana's favorite writer?

JK Rowling

92. What was Ariana's first TV show?

Victorious

93. What is Ariana's favorite candy?

Chocolate

94. Who is Ariana's best girl friend?

Victoria

95. Who is Ariana's favorite photographer?

Mario

96. What did Beyonce say about Ariana?

Powerful

97. What is Ariana's favorite TV show?

Friends

98. Fans celebrate Ariana Grande birth facts with?

Online posts

99. Ariana Grande nationality discussed in?

Recent interviews

100. What is Ariana's favorite ice cream?

Vanilla

101. What did The Weeknd say about Ariana?

Spectacular

102. Who is Ariana's celebrity crush?

Leonardo

103. Who is Ariana's favorite sibling?

Frankie

104. What is Ariana's birth lunar phase?

Full

105. Fans revisit birth info due to?

Curiosity

106. What is Ariana's favorite actor?

Leonardo

107. Ariana Grande current image is?

Private

108. Ariana Grande recalls school years as?

Formative

109. What is Ariana's favorite book?

Harry Potter

110. Her continued rise depends on?

Creative control

111. What is Ariana's birth tarot card?

The Star

112. What was Ariana's first award?

MTV

113. Fans highlight which milestone most?

Artistic evolution

114. Audiences describe Ariana Grande as?

Authentic

115. World perception of Ariana Grande is?

Evolving

116. Ariana Grande is often described as?

Dedicated

117. What did Justin Bieber say about Ariana?

Talented

118. What is Ariana's birthstone?

Diamond

119. When did Ariana's first book release?

2013

120. Recent chats show Ariana Grande was?

Driven

121. Ariana Grande avoids sharing?

Private moments

122. Her milestones confirm longevity?

Yes clearly

123. What hospital was Ariana born in?

North Shore

124. When did Ariana start her career?

2008

125. What is Ariana's most liked photo?

Dog

126. What was Ariana's first tour?

Honeymoon

127. Industry views her rise as?

Deserved

128. What was Ariana's favorite singer?

Whitney Houston

129. Fans admire her honesty about?

Personal growth

130. Ariana Grande enjoys what off stage?

Quiet time

131. What is Ariana's middle name?

Joan

132. What is Ariana's most streamed song?

Thank U Next

133. Ariana Grande gained renewed attention through?

New music

134. Ariana Grande is described as what artist?

Pop vocalist

135. What did Shawn Mendes say about Ariana?

Magnificent

136. What is Ariana's favorite holiday?

Christmas

137. Who is Ariana's favorite niece?

Nicole

138. Who is Ariana's father?

Edward

139. Fans relate to her growth because?

Honest

140. Ariana Grande birthday trends on?

Social media

141. Her global appeal comes from?

Emotional connection

142. Ariana Grande is respected for?

Artistry

143. What is Ariana's favorite ice cream?

Vanilla

144. Who is Ariana's favorite dancer?

Michael

145. What time was Ariana born?

8:45 AM

146. What is Ariana's birthdate?

June 26 1993

147. Ariana Grande birth stories appear in?

Fan discussions

148. Who is Ariana's favorite aunt?

Nicole

149. Who is Ariana's first kiss?

Graham

150. What was Ariana's first song release?

The Way

151. What was Ariana's first perfume?

Ari

152. Ariana Grande early interests included?

Performing arts

153. Who is Ariana's manager?

Scooter

154. What was Ariana's first acting award?

Best Actress

155. Ariana Grande chooses projects that are?

Personal

156. Media calls Ariana Grande?

Influential

157. What is Ariana's most retweeted tweet?

Quote

158. Who is Ariana's favorite actor?

Leonardo

159. Recent media credits her rise to?

Talent

160. Critics note Ariana Grande growth as?

Mature

161. Ariana Grande defines love with?

Care

162. Friends call Ariana Grande a?

Loyal ally

163. What did Bruno Mars say about Ariana?

Awesome

164. What did Camila Cabello say about Ariana?

Admirable

165. What is Ariana's favorite dessert?

Ice Cream

166. What is Ariana's birth Chinese element?

Water

167. What is Ariana's most famous hairstyle?

Ponytail

168. Who is Ariana's favorite painter?

Van Gogh

169. Fans say Ariana Grande laughs easily?

Yes often

170. What was Ariana's first endorsement?

Reebok

171. What is Ariana's birth lucky number?

3

172. Who is Ariana's favorite historian?

Herodotus

173. Who are Ariana's parents?

Joan & Edward

174. What was Ariana's first platinum album?

My Everything

175. Who is Ariana's favorite cousin?

Nicole

176. What is Ariana's most famous collaboration?

The Weeknd

177. Recent milestones brought Ariana Grande?

New listeners

178. Ariana Grande handles criticism with?

Reflection

179. What is Ariana's birth planet?

Mars

180. Milestones are discussed at?

Fan events

181. Who is Ariana's ex-fiance?

Pete

182. Ariana Grande keeps personal life?

Selective

183. What is Ariana's most iconic music video?

Problem

184. What did Drake say about Ariana?

Genius

185. What is Ariana's most famous tour?

Sweetener

186. What is Ariana's favorite animal?

Dog

187. What is Ariana's most sold album?

Sweetener

188. Audiences trust her creative choices?

Yes strongly

189. What was Ariana's first MTV award?

Best New Artist

190. What is Ariana's favorite animal?

Dog

191. Ariana Grande is active mainly in?

Music

192. What did Nicki Minaj say about Ariana?

Phenomenal

193. Ariana Grande birth facts remain?

Relevant

194. Who is Ariana's favorite scientist?

Einstein

195. Ariana Grande influence is strongest in?

Pop music

196. What was Ariana's first charity event?

One Love Manchester

197. What is Ariana's most awarded album?

Sweetener

198. What was Ariana's first hobby?

Singing

199. What is Ariana's birth year sign?

Monkey

200. Who is Ariana's rival?

Selena

201. What was Ariana's first performance?

School Play

202. What was Ariana's first fashion award?

Style Star

203. The world sees Ariana Grande as?

Influential

204. What did Katy Perry say about Ariana?

Strong

205. What is Ariana's favorite flower?

Rose

206. Who is Ariana's favorite uncle?

Frank

207. What was Ariana's first pet?

Dog

208. What is Ariana's favorite sport?

Swimming

209. Ariana Grande recent work focuses on?

Music projects

210. What is Ariana's birth flower?

Daisy

211. Public sees her relationships as?

Evolving

212. What is Ariana's favorite color?

Pink

213. What is Ariana's zodiac sign?

Cancer

214. What is Ariana's favorite designer?

Chanel

215. Ariana Grande is best known as?

Songwriter

216. What was Ariana's first fan club?

Arianators

217. What was Ariana's favorite activity?

Singing

218. What was Ariana's first social media post?

Selfie

219. What is Ariana's most famous quote?

Be Yourself

220. What is Ariana's favorite singer?

Whitney

221. What is Ariana's most watched interview?

Jimmy Fallon

222. What did Rihanna say about Ariana?

Inspiring

223. Who is Ariana's first boyfriend?

Graham

224. What is Ariana Grande known for today?

Singing career

225. Peers describe Ariana Grande as?

Professional

226. Who is Ariana's favorite sculptor?

Michelangelo

227. Fans respect Ariana Grande for?

Boundaries

228. What was Ariana's favorite book?

Harry Potter

229. What is Ariana's favorite hobby?

Singing

230. What is Ariana's favorite flower?

Rose

231. Who is Ariana's favorite nephew?

Max

232. What is Ariana's favorite color?

Pink

233. What is Ariana's birth year?

1993

234. What was Ariana's first live performance?

Teen Choice Awards

235. When did Ariana's first movie premiere?

2012

236. What is Ariana's favorite drink?

Water

237. Who is Ariana's favorite designer?

Chanel

238. Who is Ariana's ex-fiance?

Pete

239. What was Ariana's favorite subject?

Art

240. Ariana Grande surprises fans by?

Being candid

241. Ariana Grande symbolizes what?

Modern pop artistry

242. What is Ariana's favorite actress?

Jennifer

243. What is Ariana's birth gemstone?

Opal

244. Ariana Grande values collaboration over?

Ego

245. What was Ariana's first song?

The Way

246. Who is Ariana's godmother?

Betty

247. What was Ariana's first role?

Charlotte

248. What is Ariana's natural hair color?

Brown

249. What is Ariana Grande's last name?

Voight

250. What is Ariana's favorite food?

Pasta

251. Critics call Ariana Grande performances?

Polished

252. Ariana Grande birth details feel?

Well known

253. Ariana Grande prefers calm hobbies?

Yes

254. Ariana Grande milestones shape her?

Legacy

255. What was Ariana's favorite flower?

Rose

256. What is Ariana's most praised performance?

Grammy

257. Who is Ariana's favorite director?

Steven

258. What is Ariana's birth month?

June

259. Ariana Grande is known for being?

Supportive

260. Ariana Grande rise inspires?

Artists

261. Growing up shaped Ariana Grande focus on?

Music

262. Industry friendships are mostly?

Long term

263. Fans admire Ariana Grande for?

Consistency

264. What is Ariana's most viewed concert?

Sweetener

265. What is Ariana's most iconic outfit?

Red Dress

266. What was Ariana's favorite game?

Hide and Seek

267. Ariana Grande youth influenced her?

Vocal style

268. What did Lady Gaga say about Ariana?

Exceptional

269. What was Ariana's first instrument?

Piano

270. Where was Ariana Grande born?

Florida

271. Ariana Grande legacy is viewed as?

Enduring

272. Public says Ariana Grande is?

Focused

273. Who is Ariana's mother?

Joan

274. Fans note she supports?

Fellow artists

275. Fans say Ariana Grande vocals are?

Powerful

276. Ariana Grande childhood stories appear in?

Recent interviews

277. Who is Ariana's favorite philosopher?

Socrates

278. Fans say her fun side feels?

Natural

279. What is Ariana's birth lucky color?

Red

280. Who is Ariana's best friend?

Alexa

281. What was Ariana's first big break?

Victorious

282. What was Ariana's first school?

Pine Crest

283. What is Ariana's favorite dessert?

Ice Cream

284. Recent articles say she prioritizes?

Emotional health

285. Fans call Ariana Grande a?

Pop icon

286. Career milestones reflect her?

Growth

287. What was Ariana's first No.1 album?

Sweetener

288. Fans admire Ariana Grande for?

Consistency

289. What was Ariana's favorite vacation?

Disney World

290. Reviewers say Ariana Grande music feels?

Emotional

291. What was Ariana's first live TV performance?

Teen Choice Awards

292. Where did Ariana grow up?

Florida

293. Who is Ariana's idol?

Whitney

294. Industry views her milestones as?

Well timed

295. Ariana Grande discusses relationships in?

Careful interviews

296. What was Ariana's favorite candy?

Chocolate

297. What was Ariana's first fashion line?

AG

298. What was Ariana's first fragrance?

Ari

299. What was Ariana's first major collaboration?

Nicki Minaj

300. Who is Ariana's favorite actress?

Jennifer

Puzzle 1

ACROSS
1. Anna Paquin
2. Al Pacino
3. Ariana Grande

DOWN
1. Aaron Rodgers
2. Angelina Jolie
3. Anthony Joshua
4. Andrew Lincoln
5. Barack Obama
6. Adam Sandler

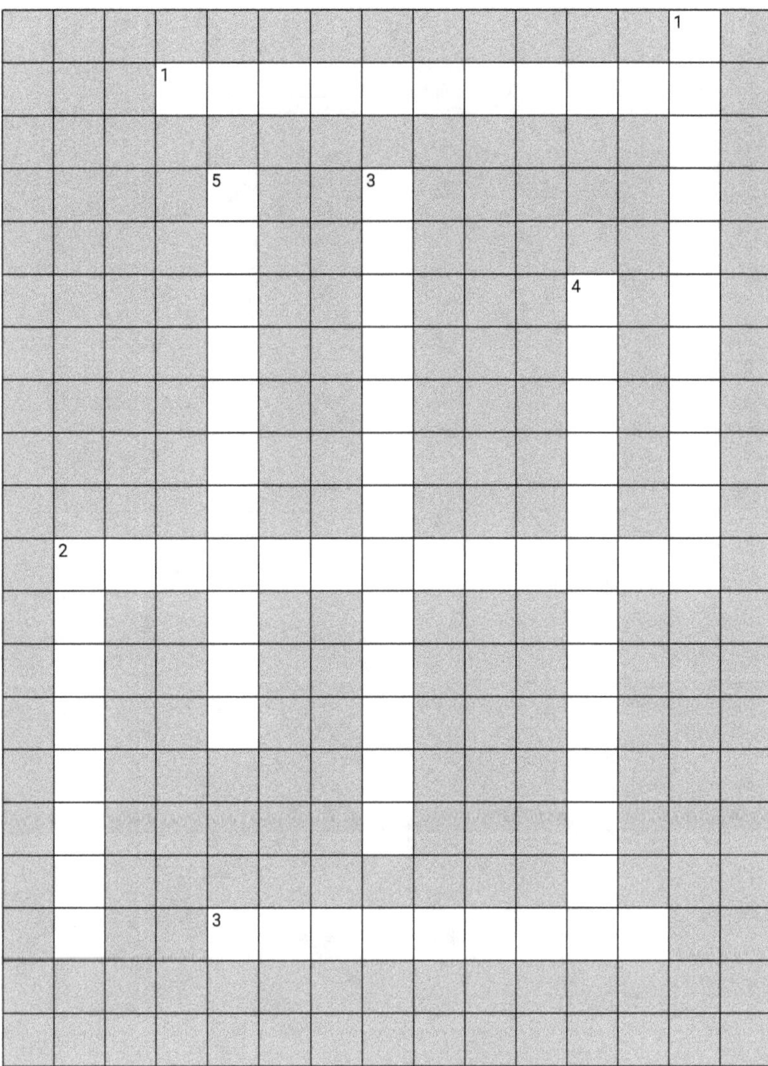

ACROSS
1. Bryce Harper
2. Bernie Sanders
3. Bruno Mars

DOWN
1. Bruce Willis
2. Brad Pitt
3. Britney Spears
4. Bradley Cooper
5. Bill Clinton

Puzzle 3

ACROSS

1. Clint Eastwood

DOWN

1. Charlize Theron
2. Cristiano Ronaldo
3. Dakota Johnson
4. Chris Evans
5. Chris Hemsworth
6. Chris Paul

Puzzle 4

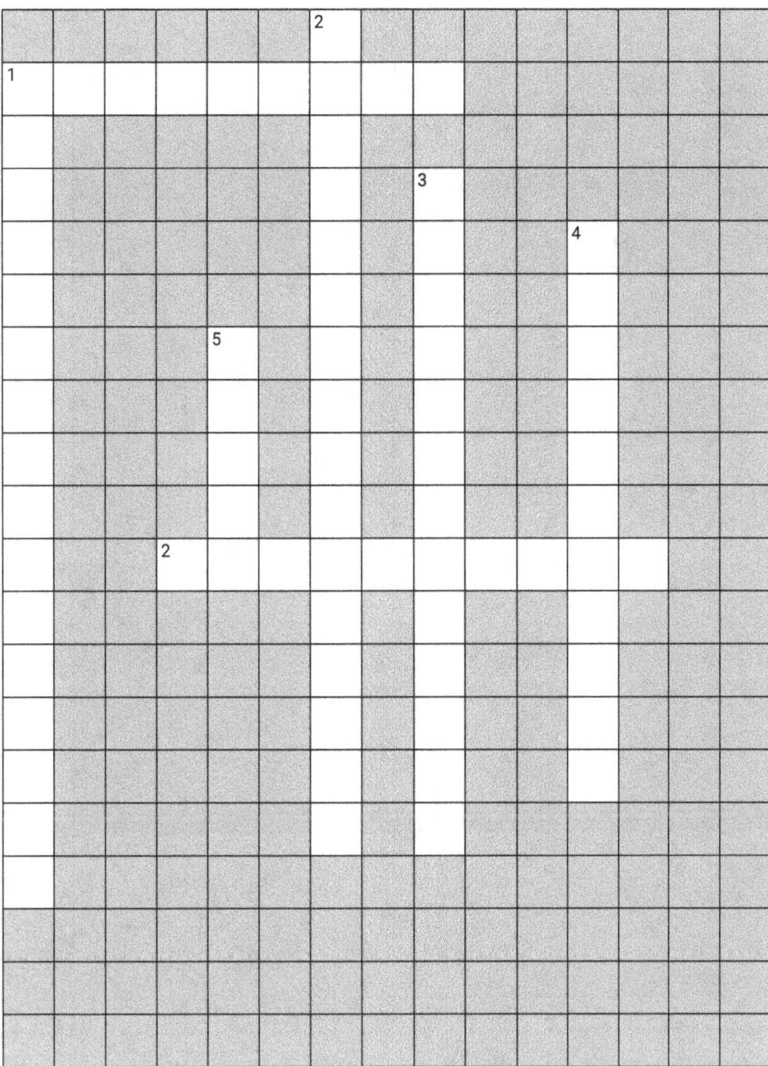

ACROSS
1. Drew Brees
2. Demi Lovato

DOWN
1. David Copperfield
2. Denzel Washington
3. Dwayne Johnson
4. Donald Trump
5. Drake

Puzzle 5

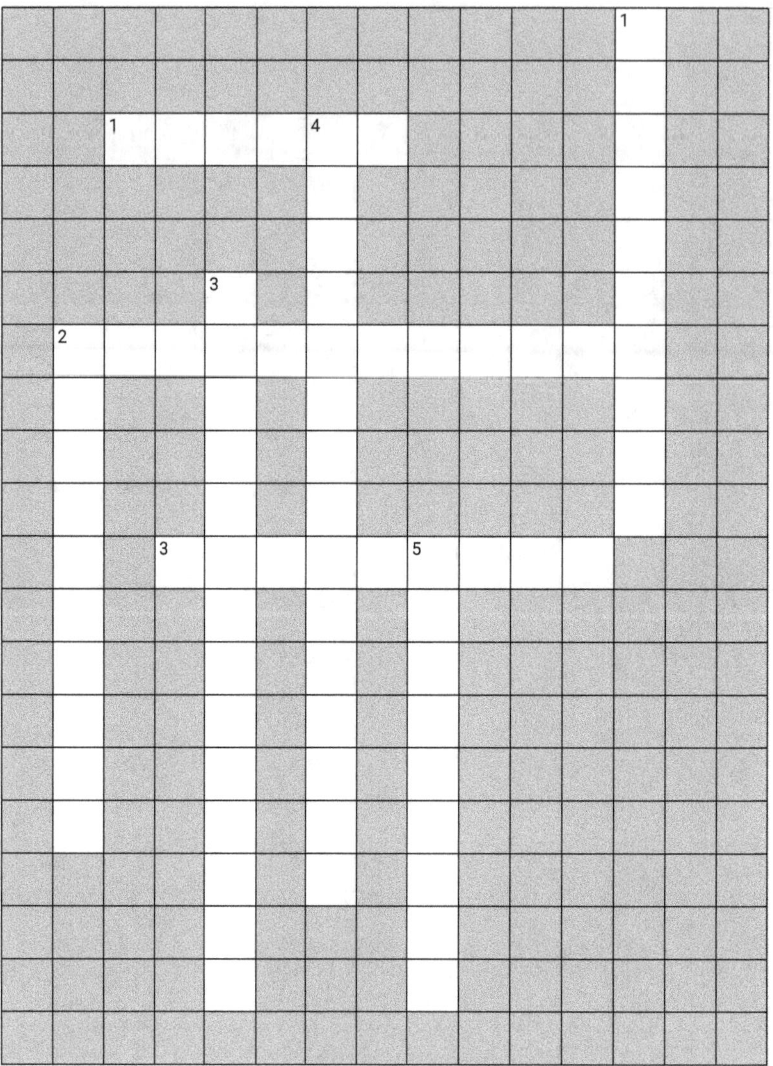

ACROSS
1. Eminem
2. Emilia Clarke
3. Ed Sheeran

DOWN
1. Halle Berry
2. Emma Watson
3. Ellen DeGeneres
4. Elizabeth Warren
5. Elton John

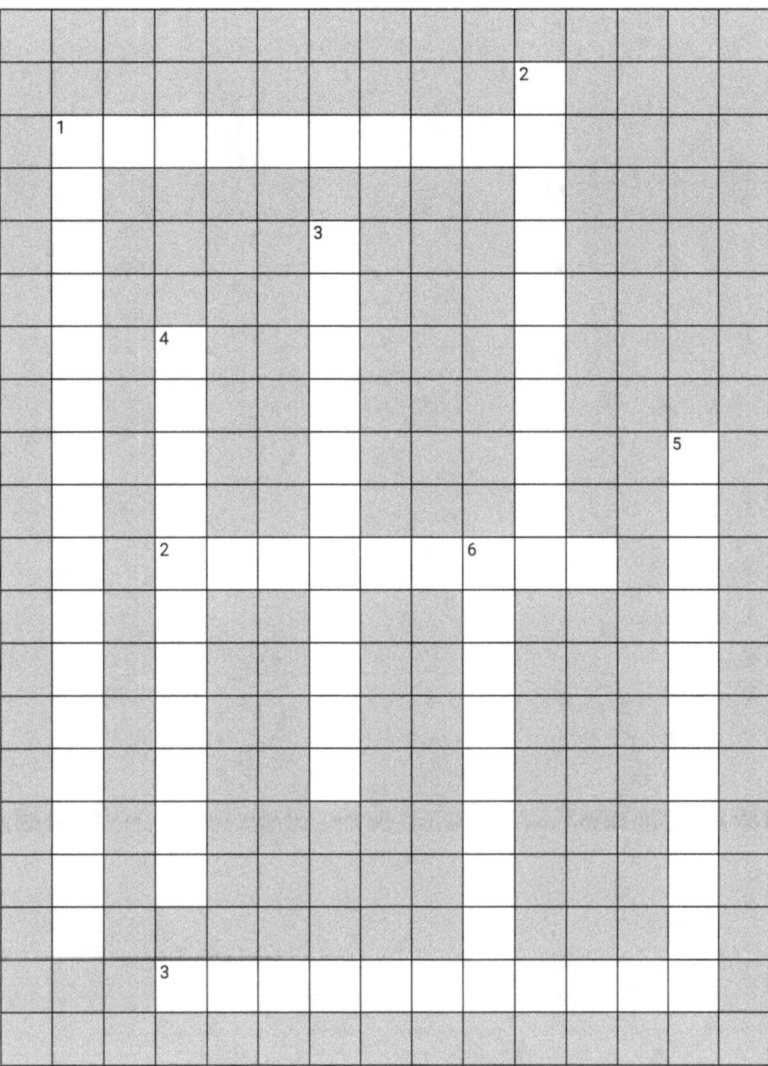

Puzzle 6

ACROSS
1. Jason Momoa
2. J.K. Rowling
3. James Harden

DOWN
1. Jada Pinkett Smith
2. Jackie Chan
3. Jamie Dornan
4. Hugh Jackman
5. Howard Stern
6. Idris Elba

Puzzle 7

ACROSS
1. Joe Biden
2. Jason Statham

DOWN
1. John Cena
2. Jeffrey Dean Morgan
3. Jennifer Lawrence
4. Jennifer Aniston
5. Jay-Z

Puzzle 8

ACROSS
1. Kendall Jenner
2. Katy Perry
3. Judy Sheindlin

DOWN
1. Justin Timberlake
2. Kanye West
3. Keanu Reeves
4. Johnny Depp
5. Justin Bieber

Puzzle 9

ACROSS
1. Kobe Bryant
2. Lady Gaga
3. Kim Kardashian

DOWN
1. Kit Harington
2. Kylie Jenner
3. LeBron James
4. Kourtney Kardashian
5. Khloe Kardashian

Puzzle 10

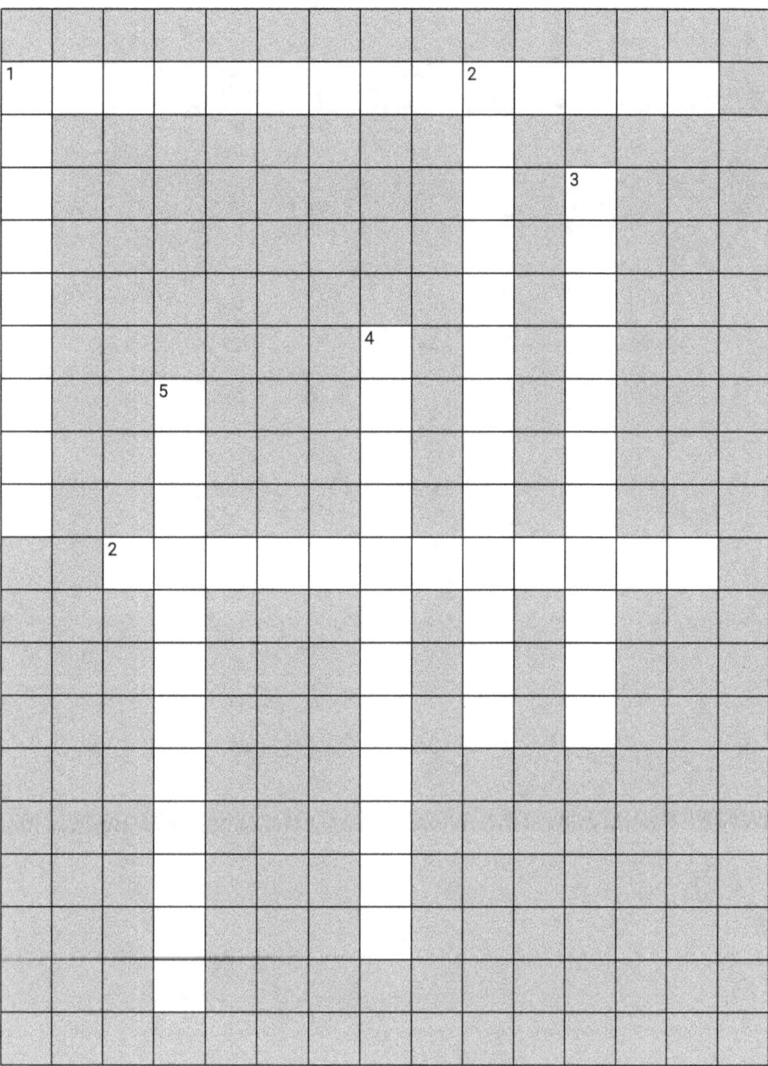

ACROSS
1. Maisie Williams
2. Mark Wahlberg

DOWN
1. Matt Damon
2. Lewis Hamilton
3. Lionel Messi
4. Meghan Markle
5. Melania Trump

Puzzle 11

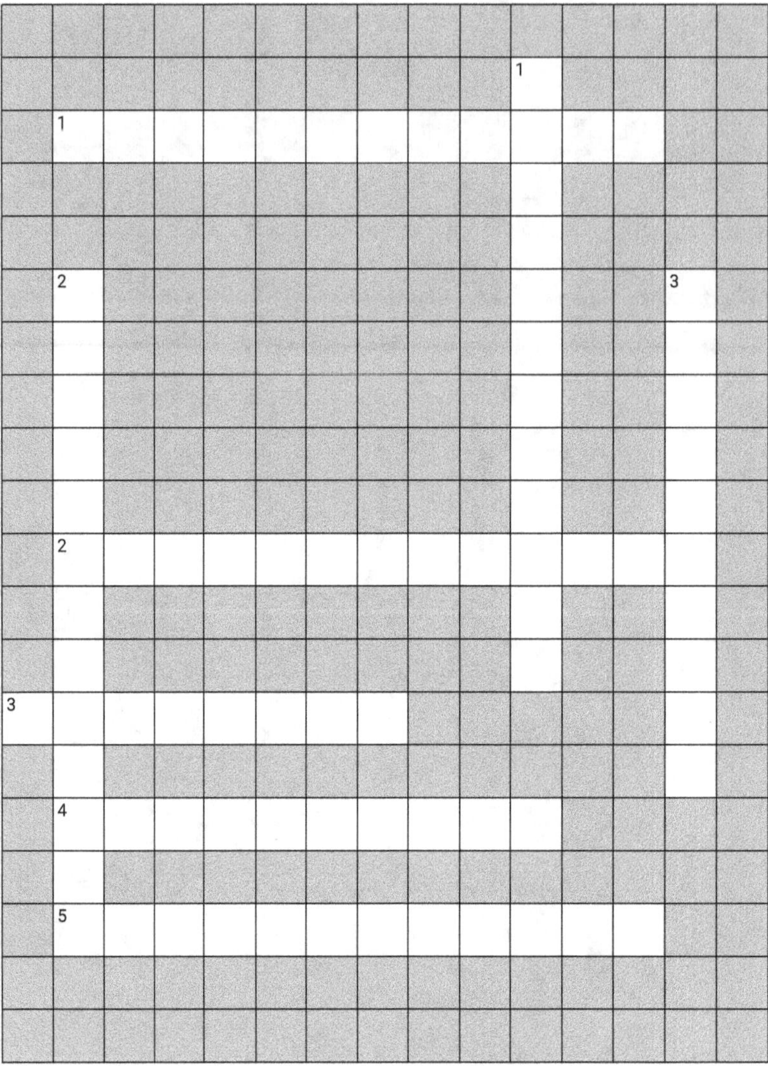

ACROSS
1. Oprah Winfrey
2. Novak Djokovic
3. Neymar Jr
4. Mitt Romney
5. Norman Reedus

DOWN
1. Orlando Bloom
2. Morgan Freeman
3. Miley Cyrus

Puzzle 12

ACROSS
1. Prince Harry
2. Pete Buttigieg
3. Pink

DOWN
1. Phil Mickelson
2. Rihanna
3. Previous Mockups
4. Peter Dinklage
5. Robert De Niro

Puzzle 13

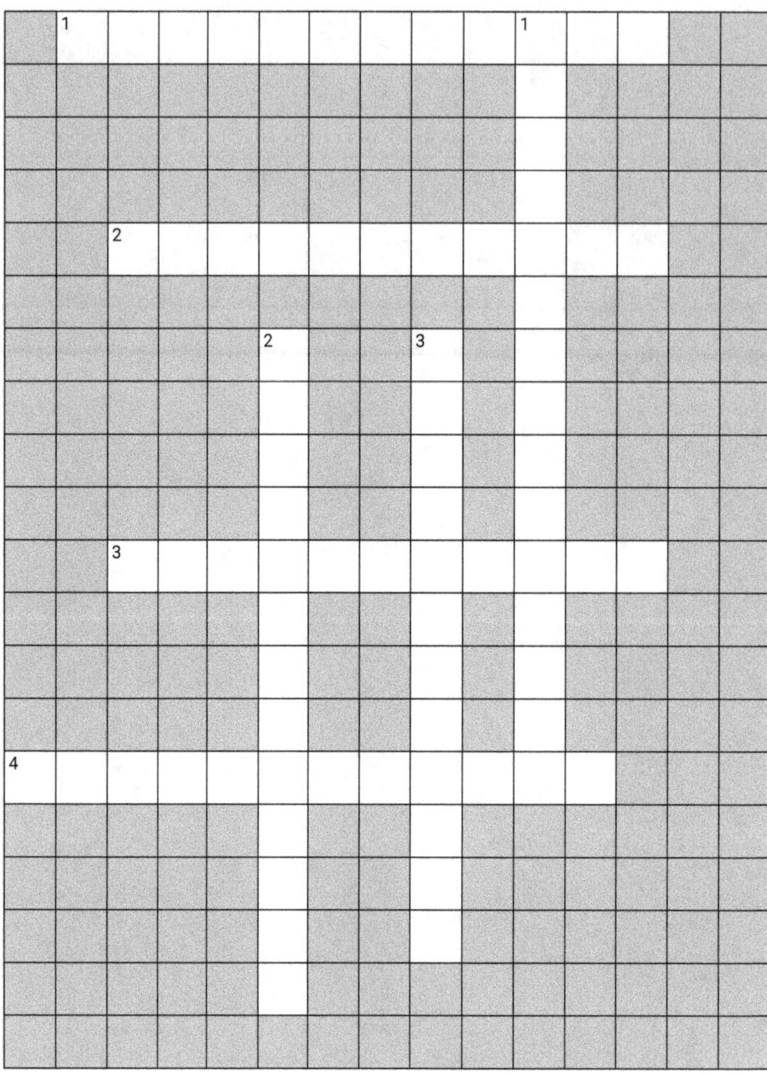

ACROSS
1. Roger Federer
2. Rory McIlroy
3. Ryan Gosling
4. Russell Brand

DOWN
1. Robert Pattinson
2. Robin Williams
3. Ryan Seacrest

Puzzle 14

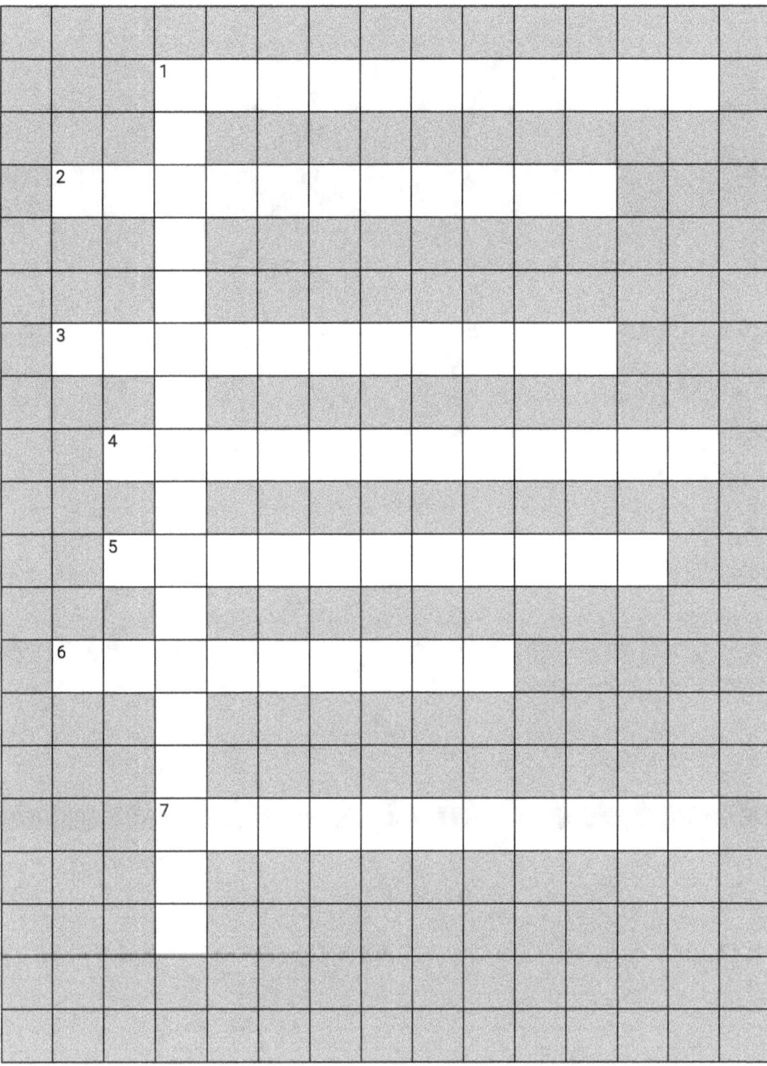

ACROSS
1. Simon Cowell
2. Shawn Mendes
3. Stephen King
4. Stephen Curry
5. Sofía Vergara
6. Sean Combs
7. Selena Gomez

DOWN
1. Scarlett Johansson

Puzzle 15

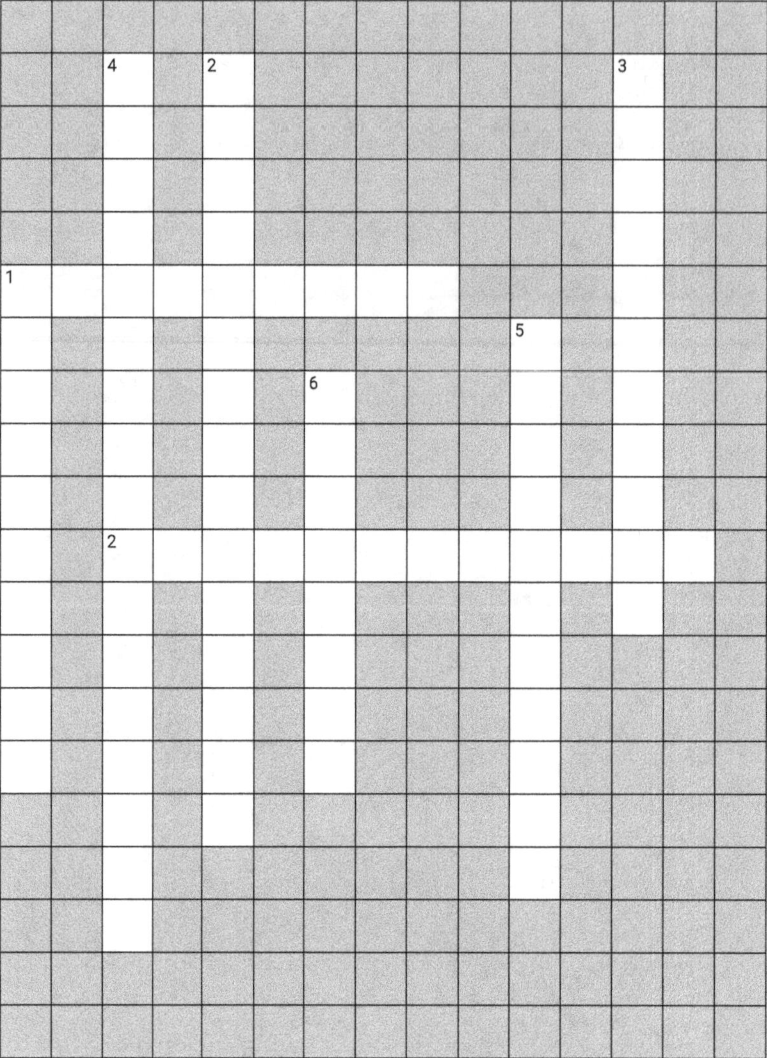

ACROSS
1. The Weeknd
2. Stephen Moyer

DOWN
1. Tiger Woods
2. Steven Spielberg
3. Steve Harvey
4. Sylvester Stallone
5. Taylor Swift
6. Tom Hanks

Puzzle 1

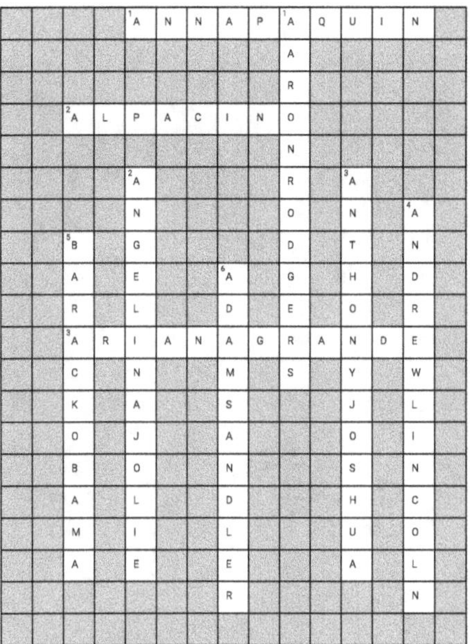

Puzzle 2

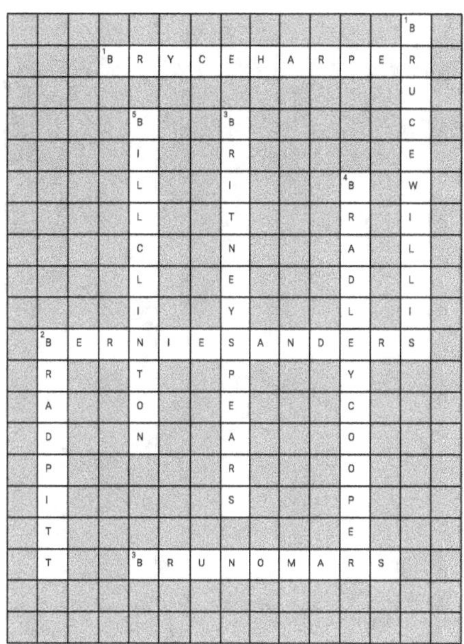

Puzzle 3

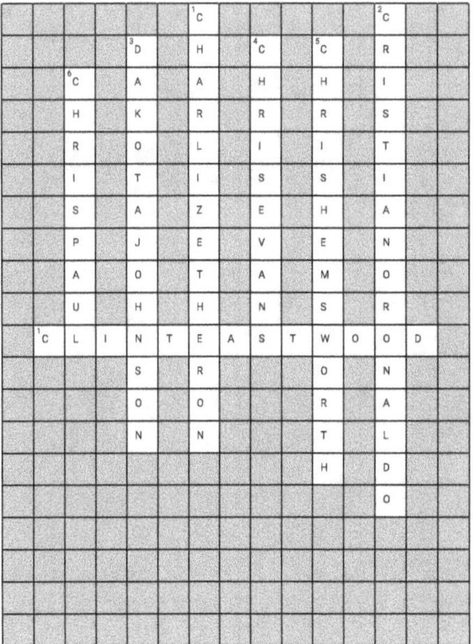

Puzzle 4

Puzzle 5

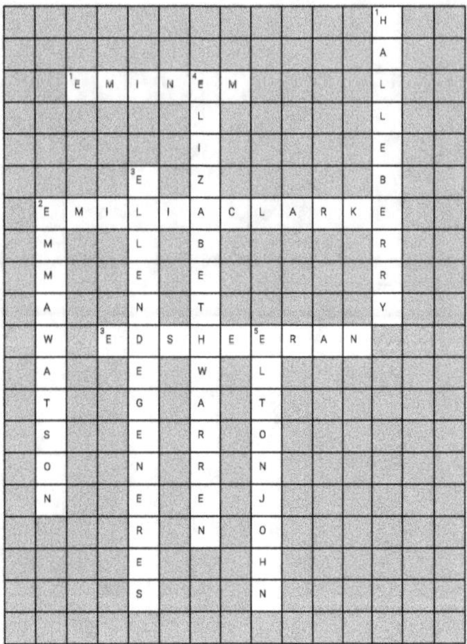

Puzzle 6

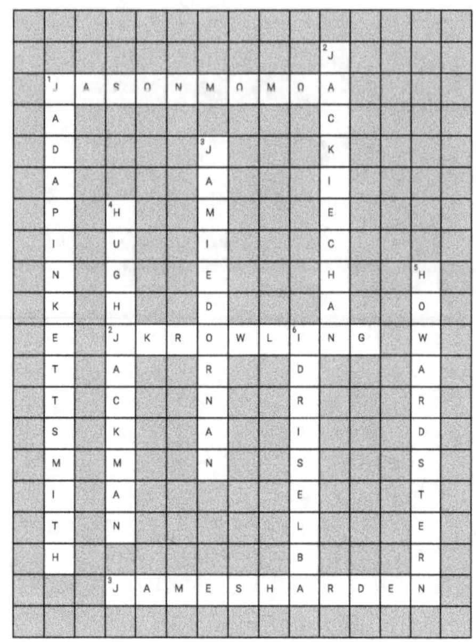

Puzzle 7

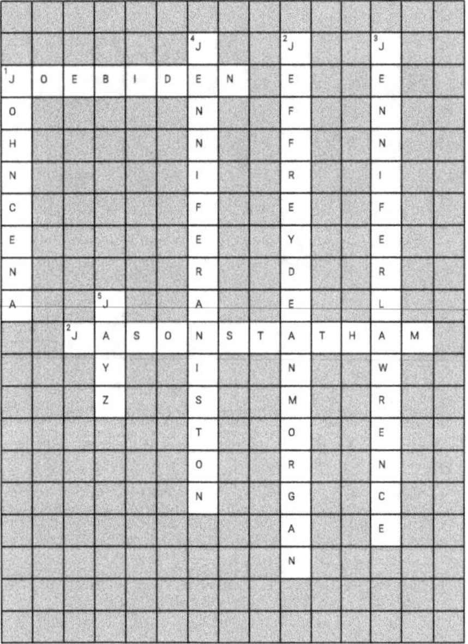

Puzzle 8

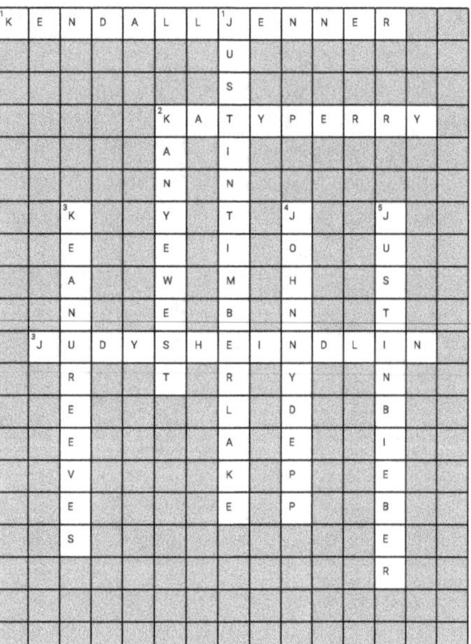

Puzzle 9

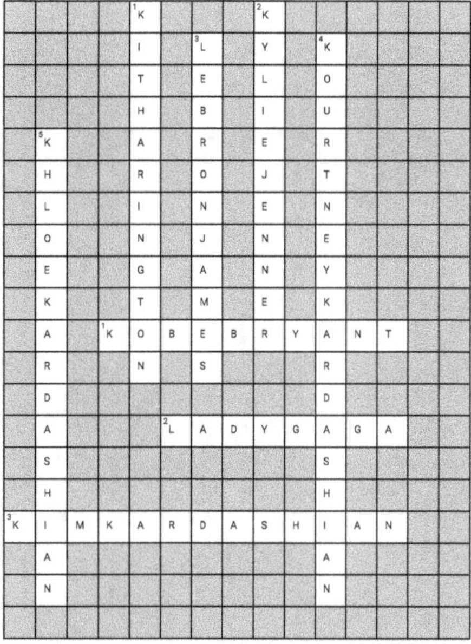

Puzzle 10

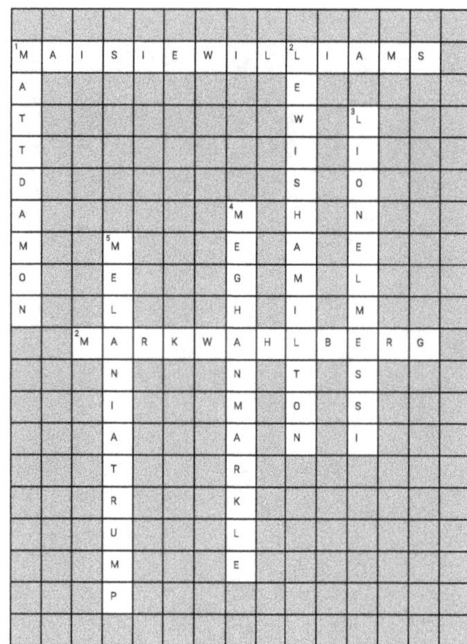

Puzzle 11

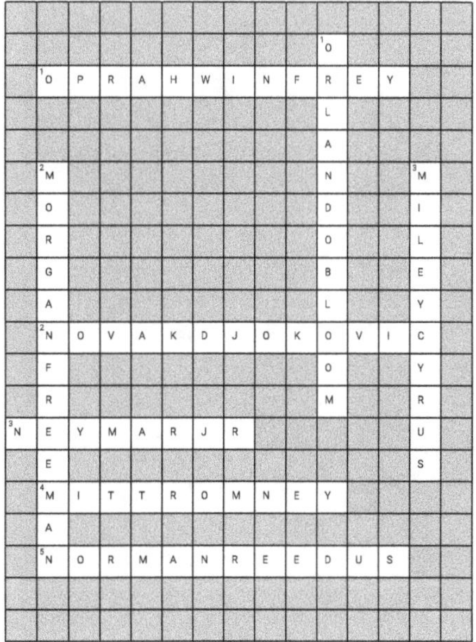

Puzzle 12

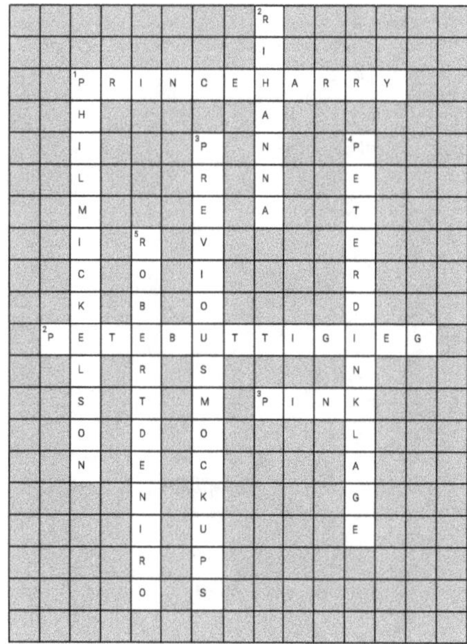

Puzzle 13

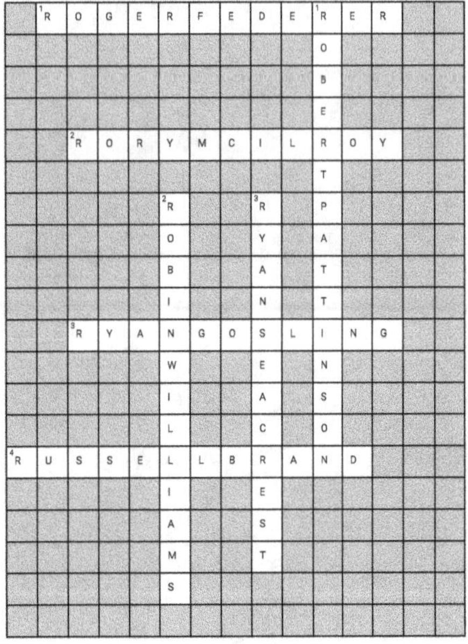

Puzzle 14

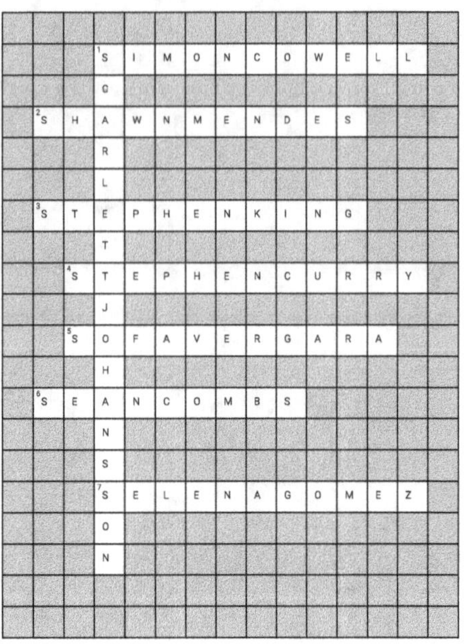

Puzzle 15